HOW TO CREATE A HEALTHY HOME BUSINESS

ANTHONY EKANEM

Copyright © Anthony Ekanem
All Rights Reserved.

ISBN 978-1-68509-026-5

This book has been published with all efforts taken to make the material error-free after the consent of the author. However, the author and the publisher do not assume and hereby disclaim any liability to any party for any loss, damage, or disruption caused by errors or omissions, whether such errors or omissions result from negligence, accident, or any other cause.

While every effort has been made to avoid any mistake or omission, this publication is being sold on the condition and understanding that neither the author nor the publishers or printers would be liable in any manner to any person by reason of any mistake or omission in this publication or for any action taken or omitted to be taken or advice rendered or accepted on the basis of this work. For any defect in printing or binding the publishers will be liable only to replace the defective copy by another copy of this work then available.

Contents

Preface v

1. Lifestyle Design 1
2. Setting Up Your Business 5
3. Discipline And Structure 13
4. Enhancing Your Health And Performance 23
5. Creating Your Home Business 27

Preface

If you run your business from home, it is important you know that you are going to be living a completely different lifestyle from the majority of the people you know. Not having to commute in the morning, not have to spend all day sitting in an office and being able to mostly create your own working hours puts you on a completely different footing from most people you know. For the most part, this is good. Being able to determine your own working hours, to dictate how and when you work, and having to spend time doing something you love, can all add to a happier and healthier lifestyle for you. In fact, it is the starting point for improving your overall health. At the same time, however, this type of lifestyle can also bring its own challenges. And because few other people would be living the same lifestyle as you, it means you are going to be somehow "on your own" when it comes to finding counsel on how to manage your work-life balance.

The long and short of it is that being self-employed and working from your home gives you the freedom to design your own lifestyle. This is the way the world is moving and it is the future of working. Technology has made it possible for people to work remotely in more industries and more roles. The benefits of this mode of working significantly outweigh the disadvantages both for the employee and the employer, and so the traditional office may soon become a rarity instead of the norm. That means the emphasis is increasingly on us to look after our own health and work-life balance. This book will help you to achieve that.

The Health Benefits of Working from Home

As mentioned earlier, when done right, working from home has incrediblehealth benefits. Let us look at the facts. Most of the population is overweight, tired and overstressed. If you can still recollect working in an office, then you will no doubt recall what it feels like to have a full day in the office, to travel home for two hours or more on the train, bus or in the car, and then have to cook dinner when you get home. What did you mostly end up doing? You threw something into the microwave and went and collapsed in front of your television. And when your friends called to invite you out, you ignored them.

Many of us talk about time management and we say that the reason we don't stick to a training regime or weight loss programme is that we don't have the time. This is not correct. Many of us have plenty of time but what we lack is energy. Without energy, we don't have willpower. Without willpower, things don't get done and we start to get drowned in a list of things we need to be doing and then we become incredibly stressed. When that happens, our bodies suffer, our relationships suffer and we don't live lives to the full. Working from home can change all of that. Working from home means that you can choose to work in the morning or in the afternoon – you just have to choose the time that is most convenient for you. At the same time, it means you can put food on the gas cooker while you are working and watch it simmer.

Working from home means that you can sit outside your home and feel the sun on your face, instead of being cooped up in an office (which is known to contribute to stress and depression). Working from home means that you do not have to commute down busy roads with many people walking at you during rush hours. This inflicts disasteron your heart rate. In short, when you work from home, you can choose your priorities and reduce the stress of working several times. Now, you can put yourself first, and that is a very important and valuable thing to be able to do.

The health benefits of working from home are enormous and life-changing. This book will show you how to start working from home if you don't already andhow to take advantage of that situation so that you are able to feel your best and reap the benefits in every other area of your life. Of course, this will have a powerful knock-on effect and impact on your productivity and help you to get more work done and to a much higher quality.

The Health Risks of Working from Home

This book will not justbe about exploiting the amazing health benefits of working from home. Just as important, we will be looking at the likely health risksthat working from home can pose. And make no mistake about it, there are many possible health risks. If you think being shouted at by your boss is stressful, how about being shouted at by 5 angry clients or 20 angry customers who just downloaded your app?

And here is the difference between working for someone compared with working for yourself: when you work for someone and you have an unproductive day, you still get paid. When you work for yourself and you have an unproductive day, you get nothing. If you have a bad month, you still get nothing. That is another thing: working for yourself is highly volatile and unpredictable and that is why some people refer to bipolar depression as 'the entrepreneur's disease'. Another difference is that when you work for yourself, your friends or relatives will not respect the fact that you have to work during the week. But when you are working from home, they can pay you a visit any time, never minding that you had promised your clients their work would be ready at some specified date and time. And on the flip side of this, your clients will not respect that your home time is your home time. They will think nothing of emailing you at 5 o'clock in the morning on a Sunday to tell you the work you delivered a few days ago was garbage.

And you will have the same problems: you will always be tempted to finish a little early on Fridays or to work a little late on Wednesdays. You will bid goodbye to the body clock! Goodbye to healthy sleep! And goodbye to good quality work. Then there is the fact that working from home means working on your own, with no one around, in the same room you are likely to spend your evening in. You never get to leave this space and you don't get any outside interaction or input.

Working from home gives you freedom, and that freedom can give you options to become exceptionally healthy, happy and effective. At the same time, however, freedom also comes with responsibility. Failure to manage that time well can make everything go wrong.

What You Will Learn

Above are a general idea and an outline of the things you will be learning in this eBook. More specifically, you will learn:

- What lifestyle design is and what it has to do with your overall health and your business
- How to apply discipline and structure when you are working from home
- How to avoid the cabin fever
- How to manage your workflow and communicate effectively with your clients and customers

- How to fit the right diet and training regime around your work
- How to sleep productively and see this impact on your productivity
- How to incorporate travel and spending time into your work
- How to transition to working for yourself
- How to generate residual income

Overall, by the end of this book, you would have the tools to create a business model and an environment that allows you to maximise your health, your happiness and productivity. If you already have a home business, you can use this guide to restructure your routine and set it up to support a happier and healthier you. If you don't already have, then use this book to give you the confidence and the know-how to take the leap in a way that will have the very best result for you.

CHAPTER ONE

Lifestyle Design

I touched briefly on the idea of lifestyle design. What does this mean exactly? The term 'lifestyle design' was either coined or made popular by Tim Ferriss in his book titled: *The Four Hour Workweek*. The idea behind it is that you create the lifestyle that you want out of your job. This means that you think about the lifestyle you want and then you choose a career or build a business to support that lifestyle. For most of us, this works in the completely opposite way.

Many of us will find ourselves 'landing in a job' and from there, we see the rest of our lifestyles forming around it. We get a job, and right away, that job dictates where we are going to live, so we normally move to that area. At the same time, it tells us which hours we are going to work and depending on how far away we live, this will also have to include the time for a commute. Some people will move away from their friends and family so they can do the job they have or will even break up relationships that were otherwise going well – all because of their job! And don't get confused; these are not jobs that they have always wanted. These are not the 'dream careers' that they have been thinking about since a young age. No, these are jobs that they 'just landed in' and are now too afraid to leave.

And the jobs are completely dictating their lives.

Lifestyle Design: The Alternative

So how does lifestyle design really work in principle? You start out by asking yourself: *"What type of life do I want?"* And from there, you ask what type of job would best facilitate that lifestyle. If you want to spend more time with your family, if you want to work while travelling, if you want to have a career that you find fascinating and that you are proud of, then the first step to achieving the right lifestyle will be to start to work for yourself and online from home.

Next, you have to ask whether you want to be a busy 'high flier' or whether you would be happier as someone whose career was 'light', flexible and would largely run itself on autopilot a lot of the time. This is an important point. Many people make the mistake of thinking they want to be 'really successful' in the most stereotypical sense and as such, they create business plans that involve taking on large numbers of staff with branches all over the place. The reality of being involved in this form of business is that you now have no time to do things that contribute to a happy and healthy life. Similarly, you are now just as stressed and as tied down, if not more so, than you would have been if you were working for a big organisation in an office.

If you *want* to be a high profile businessman or woman, that is great. If not, you need to rethink your business plan. If you want to take it even further in the *other* direction and live a relaxed lifestyle, then ideally you want some kind of passive income, meaning that you can generate money while you are asleep. This might mean selling a digital product or it might mean hiring a manager to run the day-to-day components of your business. Either way, a business that 'runs itself' allows you to live the kind of life you want and to reap the full rewards for your hard work later on.

Digital Nomad or Digital Homebody

Perhaps one of the ultimate expressions of lifestyle design is to become a digital nomad. To many people, these two terms are synonymous and interchangeable. A digital nomad is someone who works online so they are not dependent on a physical location for their career and income. They are free to go ahead with their lifestyle design, but rather than just being content to spend more time at home, they aim bigger and travel the world. The typical image of a digital nomad is someone sitting by a huge waterfall in the middle of nowhere, typing on their laptop. Or perhaps, it is of someone sitting on the beach, sipping cocktails and firing off e-mails to their clients.

This is of course highly appealing for many of us and is definitely a way of living that is more 'free' than what many of us are used to. This way, you can see the world, meet new people and take each day as it comes, never knowing where you are going to end up. That is an exciting prospect and it can lead to a healthy attitude to life for many of us. However, it is also not for *everyone*. Why? Because for starters, you will be travelling with just a backpack and you will not get the chance to have a proper bath and change to fresh clothes that you washed. Likewise, if you are partial to a cup of tea or coffee with milk, good luck getting it. Also, you cannot have a pet dog. You will be away from your friends and family and it will be scary. Travelling permanently can be very stressful *in itself* and you will spend a lot of time in dubious hostels worrying about your laptop. But you must not take an 'all or nothing' approach to be a digital nomad. Instead, you can travel the world in short bursts. Or you can go on lengthy vacations. Or you can do three holidays a year instead of one.

Travelling is not that expensive any longer, depending on which part of the world you live in. If you fly a short distance, you can go to some exotic places for $50 and if you are smart about when and how you buy, you can also travel a long distance on the train relatively cheap. While you are travelling, you can be working on your computer and that means you can earn some or all of your money back. Remember too that you can travel during the "quiet times" when everyone else is at work, meaning quiet resorts and lower prices.

Then, you can be working in a lodge in Spain, or at your friend's house in Japan. And you can do this for four or five days, several times a year and still feel like you are getting to experience more of life than your office-bound friends. At the same time, however, when you start to miss home, you can travel back and cuddle up with your spouse and children. With smart lifestyle design, you can have your cake and eat it!

CHAPTER TWO

Setting Up Your Business

This chapter is going to be aimed primarily at those who choose *not* to go the digital nomad route. Either you are someone who is content to just have more freedom working from home, or you are working from home part of the time and travelling when opportunities present themselves. Either way, the rest of the time you are going to need somewhere to work and you are going to need some structure. If you are already working from home, then you should read this chapter carefully and perhaps modify some of your current routines and setup. If you are planningon working from home, then you should use this when creating your business model and the bounds for your productivity.

Your Work Environment

Before you can start working from home, the first question you need to ask yourself is *where* you will actually be working from. In other words, where will you be physically located as you type and answer emails? Remember that we are focused on creating a lifestyle and a business model that will support good health, happiness and productivity. *Where* you are working from is a big part of this and being able to decide on the details of your work environment is one of the big advantages of working for yourself. So make the most of it!

Working From Home, But Not From Home

The first point to note here is that working from home does not have to *mean* working from home. We have already seen that when we discussed becoming a 'digital nomad' in the previous chapter. You can take a similar approach locally too, by just taking a laptop with you and working from local coffee shops or libraries. This has a lot of advantages as compared with working from an office in your own home. For starters, when you work from a coffee shop, you get to leave the house. This is significant because it psychologically separates your work life from your home life and makes it a little easier for you to 'switch off' when you get home. At the same time, it also means that you will be taking some steps. It is recommended that you take several steps a day, and failing to do so is bad for your heart, which may lead to obesity, back problems or even a shorter life.

Another benefit is that this way, you will get to meet people. Again, this is an important point to make because spending all your time at home can leave you feeling a little restless and is not healthy. By going to a coffee shop, on the other hand, you will get to be aroundother people who are working and you will get to interact with the people who work there. If you want to go a step further, you can look for a shared workspace. There are many of these kinds of initiatives around these days, especially in larger towns and cities. Not only do these offer you the chance to get out of the house, but you will also get to spend time with people who are there doing something similar to yours. This creates networking opportunities and further means that the working environment will be entirely geared towards the kind of work you are doing. That means you will get good Wi-Fi and peace and quiet as standard. Some shared workspaces even give you your own telephone line and Post Office Box.

There are other options too, for example, you could always go to a quiet hotel or even a bar, or you could sit outside when the weather is pleasant. Sitting outside is, of course, great from a health angle but unfortunately is rather lacking in terms of expediency and convenience. To do this well, you will need to contend with glare on the screen, the lack of space to sit and prop your laptop, bugs, dirt, grass and lack of power or Wi-Fi. Still, there may be somewhere near you that is responsible for all this. Maybe you have a drink with someone outside seating that is quiet during the day and faces the beach. The world is your home when you "work from home".

Setting Up a 'Mobile Command Center'

If you are going to work wherever you like (or become a digital nomad), then you must have something to work *with*. Any small laptop will do the magic and should slip neatly into a shoulder bag or a backpack. You may be limited by the operating system you can use but if not, the MacBook Airs are *particularly* light and convenient as are Chromebooks. For Microsoft Windows users, the Surface Pro 3 is a *fantastic* machine. This device is basically a tablet with a slim keyboard built into its cover. It works on your lap and weighs barely anything. What is more? It has a beefy specification, neat features and a long battery life. The 'Surface 3' (apart from the 'Pro') is also very good, being a little smaller and cheaper but on an Atom processor.

If you want something lighter, you can go a step further and consider one of the many Windows tablets. With one of these plus a portable Bluetooth keyboard and mouse, you can do anything you can do on a small Ultrabook and never feel weighed down. They have about 1-2GB RAM, very long batteries. That means you can take them on a vacation and not worry *too* much about anything happening to them. You can even *combine* a Surface Pro 3 with an 8" tablet and use it to extend your screen – now you have a multi-monitor setup even in a coffee shop! It looks very silly and it is great for real productivity on the move.

Creating Your Home Office

You might decide that you reallywant to work from home. This is fine but you must be strict about the way you are going to do it to ensure you maintain a separation between your home life and your work life and to maintain good health. The first tip is to make sure that your home office is really a home office and not just a table in your sitting room. And do notwork in your bedroom. In fact, the ideal situation is that you *only* use your bedroom for sleeping and for sex. That way, when you head into your bedroom, your body and mind will automatically start winding down for sleep. If you spend part of your day working in the room, you will find it is hard to switch off, even when you are under the covers.

For the above reasons, you must choose a different room or space in your house to be your home office. This way, you can create that separation and it will also mean you are less likely to be disturbed when working from home while your family and other people are in the house. Soundproofing is clearly ideal but not necessary. The next important thing to think about when making your home office is lighting. Some people actually create 'office pods' these days at the end of their garden, which are mostly glass sheds that allow them to work as if they were being surrounded by nature. You don't have to go that far. Just provide adequate light in the room where you will be working.

Large windows and lots of house plants have been shown to help fight depression and stress. Having a 'natural' view can boost creativity by lowering our heart rate and allowing our minds to wander. Another important way to maintain good health is to consider the way you will be sitting. This means making sure that you are upright, with your back well supported by the chair. You should position your computer monitor so that it is approximately the same height as your eyes with your chin parallel to the floor. If you are looking down all day, you will develop rounded shoulders and kyphosis.

Your hands should be hovering above your computer keyboard and you should be high enough that your elbows are at a right angle as you type. If you want to optimize your home office for maximum health benefits, you should also consider getting a standing desk. A good standing desk designs use a collapsing frame that allows you to work either sitting *or* standing. It can be hard to concentrate for a long time while standing, so you might be unable to do this the whole time. However, when you are answering e-mails or doing something with design software, standing up can give your back a real break and can help you to burn more calories at the same time.

As for the rest of your home office design, you can go ahead and decorate it the way you like. The more colours, the more life, and the more points of interest, the better. While you might think this sounds distracting, it actually makes your environment richer from a psychological standpoint and that has been linked to triggering a 'flow state' which is a state of intense concentration and high productivity. The more engaging your environment, the more adrenaline and dopamine you will produce and the more focused you will be at all times.

Some Health Tips for Working at a Computer

Regardless of whether you are working from a beach in Dubai, or from a home office, or at your local coffee shop, there are health considerations you need to bear in mind which can make a big difference.

Move Regularly

Sitting correctly at the desk, or getting a standing desk can both help you to avoid some of the drawbacks of sitting at a desk all day. Just move around several times and that way, you will avoid seizing up and you will be trying out different positions. If you have a home office, then you should invest in a comfortable chair and desk. But likewise, you should also give yourself some alternative places to work whether that is a sofa or a beanbag in the corner of the room. Now you will have the option of switching your positions in the room whenever you become uncomfortable. Also important is to get up every hour or so, even if it is for ten minutes. All these can help to prevent the weakening of your hamstrings, poor posture, back and knee pains as well as poor mobility. Moreover, it will help prevent the atrophy of your heart which can significantly shorten your lifespan.

Get a Mechanical Keyboard

If you are typing a lot on a daily basis, you open yourself up to repetitive strain injury, arthritis and other issues. A mechanical keyboard can help you to avoid these problems, by giving you something to type on that is specifically designed to be ergonomic, comfortable and supportive. A good mouse will make a big difference also.

Consider Dvorak

Dvorak is an alternative keyboard layout to QWERTY that is said to be more efficient. It puts all the most commonly used letters in the easiest-to-reach positions and this, in turn, can speed up typing and at the same time reduce the risk of arthritis. It takes a while to learn and the research surrounding Dvorak is not concrete. Nonetheless, if the idea appeals to you, then give it a try and you may find it helpful.

Avoid the Screen at Night

If you are going to be working late into the night, which you may do despite your best intentions, you should consider using software to redden the screen, or maybe try wearing some 'blue-blocking' glasses. Regrettably, the nature of the wavelength of light produced by most computer monitors is such that the brain mistakes it for sunlight and reacts by producing more cortisol and less melatonin. This makes it hard for you to sleep and leaves you restless throughout the night; so use these two techniques to avoid that problem.

Protecting Your Eyes

Do you sometimes find yourself wishing you didn't have to look at a computer screen all the time? Does it give you a headache or make you worry about your eyesight? The good news is that looking at a computer screen is not actuallybad for your eyes. Studies found that people who sat closer to the computer or TV had worse eyesight but they had the correlation the wrong way – people sat closer to the computer or television screen *because* of their *pre-existing* poor eyesight. In fact, playing a computer game actually improves your visual acuity by forcing you to be aware of your environment.

The only danger that comes from looking at computer screens is caused by glare and changes in brightness. It is going from a very bright screen to a dark object in the room or going from a text with a glare to text without the glare that forces the eyes to work hard and readjust its focus. This can wear out the eyes muscles and that iswhen you have headaches. Therefore, make sure that you work to avoid glare. If you are will be working on-the-go, make sure your computer has a flexible hinge to avoid direct light and choose your spot wisely. If you are working from home, make sure you have no windows or lamps in front of the screen. Keep the room you are working in well-lit and if itgets darker, turn the brightness of your monitor down too. Do this and you would have no reason to worry about your eyes while working from home.

CHAPTER THREE

Discipline and Structure

If you take and apply all the advice in the last chapter, you should now have a conducive working environment that is good for your health, and you should know how to avoid some of the common risks of working from home and with the computer. What you still need to do is to think about the psychologicalaspect of your work and the way you are mentally separating one from the other. This is where many people who work from home get it wrong. We start out with good intentions (set working hours, create our home-office, get a separate work phone) but the temptation to work late nights, or to work on weekends and public holidays, will always rear its ugly head once we start getting behind.

The problem is that it is habit-forming, and it creates a bad pattern. This is particularly true if you work late on weekdays, as you will have less energy to work again on the nextworkday and that in turn will mean you are tired, lethargic and unproductive, which means there is a good chance you will be tempted to work late again. As we shall see later, sleep should be considered sacred if you work from home. And for everybodyfor that matter.

What you need to do is to set for yourself specific parameters for working and to notwork outside of those parameters. This means that you have to startworking from a specific time and end at a specific time. And what if you run over and work looks like it is going to be late? Then you have to accept that it is late. It is not worth ruining your life to make a client happy. Remember that the major reason we are working this way is to live the lifestyle that we want.

Of course, it is good that you keep your clients happy, and this is where time management comes in – and generally taking the right approach when managing your clients and knowing how to accept work and handle different projects. You also need to put measures in place that will help you manage your workflow and to become scalable even as an individual. And guess what? That is what we will be looking at in the rest of this chapter. Continue reading.

Accepting Work

The big challenge as an entrepreneur or any kind of sole trader is trying to find work. Dry spells are devastating when you have huge bills to pay and the family is telling you to go and 'get a real job' and if you run a service-based business, no order means no money. But what is alsoa big challenge is learning to say 'no' when it is necessary to say so. Learn to turn down clients, or to tell them they can have the work delivered in a week. We are often afraid to do this because we don't want to be in a situation where we have no work to do, and as a result, we end up taking on more than we can chew and working odd hours that prevent us from sleeping well at night. Worst of still, the work you deliver probably won't be as good as it should be because you would have been rushed.

So sometimes, you have to be firm and tell your client it would be a few days before you can get the work to them. That is fine, in fact, it is very normal. As long as you tell them up-front how long it would take for you to deliver, you don't need to feel bad about it. Do your job very well and your clients should be able to wait (unless their work is time-bound also). If it is a web design, some SEO, an article writing, a couple of days likely would not make much difference to their business plan.

The same goes for turning down work that you are not confident about or that you really do not want to do. Just tell your client that there are other service providers that will do a better job for less money instead of killing yourself trying to learn a completely new skill set. Be firm about what you do and do them very well. You will be happy, your life will be simpler, and the quality of your work will be high.

And in fact, when you tell your clients or customers how long your work is going to take, you should actually be pessimistic about it. This is known as 'under-promising and over-delivering' and it means saying that things will take longer, cost more, be worse and then providing a pleasant surprise. This strategy is great from a business standpoint because it gives you the opportunity to impress your clients, which leads to a memorably positive interaction that will make them more likely to want to use your services again and again. What is more? Under promising means that if things go wrong and you cannot finish the work as quickly as you should, you will still have some time to get your work delivered on time. It is a simple strategy that will greatly reduce the amount of stress that you go through.

And if you are concerned you would not get many orders this way, you can always give an 'expected completion time' and a 'promised completion time' as separate offers. Bear in mind that you cannot rule out the possibility of delivering your work late. There will be times when things come up unexpectedly. It is important to remember that you would not get any paid sick leave as a self-employed person. With that said, you should not be afraid to occasionally 'phone in sick' with clients as it is more efficient in the long term.

Choosing Clients

Sometimes you need to turn down work that you are offered, or just say you are handing it in late. Other times, however, you can turn down clients. That is because there is a 'good client' and a 'bad client'. Bad clients are the ones who produce too much 'communication overhead' (meaning they call and e-mail you all the time about petty things, eventually costing you time and money). They are also the ones who make a payment late (or not at all) and who are often not satisfied with your work. You will find that some of your clients fit this description, while others are polite and send a minimum number of e-mails and make fewer phone calls necessary for you to work.

It is the latter kind you want to work with as it will eventually save you time and stress down the line. Again, picking and choosing your clients is one of the big benefits when it comes to working for yourself. Another type of client you perhaps want to lose is the one who orders small amounts of work. The more small clients you have, the more relationships you would have to manage, the more projects you would have to order and largely the more stressed you are likely to be. This is called the 'Pareto's Law' or the '80/20' rule. The notion is that it is about 20% of your customers who provide about 80% of your revenue – and that you should focus on that 20% instead of the other 80%.

Revenue Streams

Try and avoid a situation where you put all your eggs in one basket. In other words, if you turn down allyour clients and end up with just one, then you are going to be in a sticky situation if that one client suddenly quits. The ideal situation is to spread your workload. And in terms of income, you should be able to survive relatively well even if you lose someof those clients. The same applies if you are selling a product from your website, or if you are selling an app ... have multipleapps and multiple products.

It is even a good idea to have a completely separate revenue stream. Let's say you are a web designer with numerous big clients. As a designer, you might go some lengthy patches where you do not have any work coming in and as such, you should make sure you have a monetized website, an app or something else that is bringing in extra money. You could even leave your home for a few days and offer your services as a painter by driving around the neighbourhood. In other words, you need as many income streams as possible. You need backup plans and contingencies. With all these in place, you will be less reliant on steady work and you will, therefore, be less tempted to take on more work than you can manage during busy periods.

Another tip is to use your "quiet days" to put work in ahead of time. For example, if you are a web designer, you can always try designing some unique fonts or some website templates that you can use later on to save your time. This way, you will be able to take on more work later on, without being overwhelmed.

Targets

While doing all the work, it may be useful to set targets for yourself in terms of how much you want to earn. Do not aim too high but make sure that it is something you can realistically live off. Depending on the nature of your work, something like $200 per day is a good 'base rate'. Having a target like this is good because it allows you to structure every other thing accordingly and to decide how much work you are willing to take on and at what time in the week you are going to do it. At the same time, you can be sure that you will be sticking to a minimum amount of income without going broke.

Systems

Even with a good number of clients and no unreal expectations, you will probably still find that things can get out of hand and you can be stressed. When your clients send you messages at 8.00 PM on a Friday night saying that the work you did for them is not good, how can you ignore that? Similarly, when it turns out the software update you released to your customers had a major bug in it on Friday night, again, what can you do?

There are different systems and tools that you can put in place to help you in any of these situations. If you want to find out more about these, I recommend *'The Four Hour Workweek'* by Tim Ferriss which discusses this sort of thing in-depth. However, the ones discussed below should be enough to help you significantly reduce your stress, working from home, so you can start improving your health and happiness.

Auto-Responders

The first and most straightforward tool to use is your e-mail autoresponder. This allows you to send an automated reply to your clients, customers and business partners whenever they send you a message after a particular time or on a weekend, and it can be configured to say something like: *"Thank you for your message. I'm afraid I will be out of the office until tomorrow at 9.00 AM and will be unable to respond until then. If you have an emergency, you can contact me on my home phone number 123456789. But please don't call if it can wait until tomorrow. My working hours are between 9.00 AM and 6.00 PM Monday to Friday."* This e-mail is perfect because it tells your clients or customers why you have not gotten back to them and gives them the means to get in touch if they are in a dire situation. You will find that very few people will actually abuse your home number, so you can be safe in the knowledge that you will be undisturbed. With that said, you can stop imagining worst-case scenarios.

Virtual Assistants

A virtual assistant is somebody who can handle different types of work on your behalf as long as they do not need to be physically present. Generally, these companies or individuals are based in India or other countries with lower costs of living, so you will probably only pay a few dollars for a day's work. Of course, you get what you pay for to an extent, so do not expect incredible English unless you are willing to pay more dollars.

Either way, these companies or individuals provide work that can include: booking appointments, responding to e-mails, doing research, marketing and SEO, proofreading, data entry and so much more. You can use a digital assistant to outsource the boring or time-consuming aspects of your job, while you focus on doing what you do well. Virtual assistants can also stand in for you on weekends. Similarly, it does not hurt to know people who can help you out in a crisis. If you have a friend who also works online, you can make an agreement with them to bail each other out occasionally if you have too much work. You might even be able to offer some aspects of your work to friends who are interested in making extra money on the side!

Automation

There are different tools you can use online to automate your work. One of such tools is IFTTT (which stands for 'If This, Then That') allows you to link different online tools and social media accounts together. For instance, IFTTT - https://ifttt.com can create a system where your Facebook posts are also posted to Twitter. This can save you a lot of time in a social media campaign. You can also use this tool to copy all your Gmail contacts to a Google Drive spreadsheet or to add Google Calendar appointments to a To-Do List. IFTTT and many other tools like it can act as force multipliers and save you a *lot* of time.

A Separate Phone

If you use your mobile phone for work, it is advisable to have a *separate* mobile phone for your personal life. This way, you can drop the work mobile phone in a drawer at the end of the working day. By so doing, you will not be disturbed by e-mails from your clients, or from customers or visitors to your website, because you won't be aware of them.

Hypothesis Testing

All these tools will do a lot to help you spend less time working and help you 'switch off' at the end of the day. Ultimately, you are still going to have to 'trust' in the fact that you can take time off work or not respond immediately to an e-mail, and this is the hard part. It is also the crucialpart though. Until you learn to psychologicallylet go of work, you are not going to get the recovery you need to be healthy and to perform optimally.

Even if you are not getting e-mails, you will still find that work takes its toll if you are lying away thinking about how to apologize to an angry client who has sent you an e-mail. The best way to accomplish this is with a cognitive behavioural therapy technique called 'hypothesis testing'. Here, you think about the thing you are afraid to do and you think about what it is that is making you afraid to do it. You may be afraid to ignore e-mails or turn down work because you think your clients will leave you.

To let go of that fear, trynot to responding to e-mails sometimes. Give it a go – respond to the next e-mail you get tomorrowinstead of right now and then apologize for being late. In all likelihood, you will find there are no repercussions and as a result, you will be more inclined to do the same thing again next time. Similarly, trynot to update your website for a week and see whether it hurts your traffic that much.

Your Personal Life

Most of what we have discussed so far has revolved around designing your work so it does not interfere with your personal life. But for this to be effective, it has to work both ways and you have to make sure your personal life is not interfering with your work. That, in turn, means that you have to be firm when it comes to not taking calls, or meeting with friends during your working hours. And just as you put your work phone in a drawer in the evenings, you should also consider putting your home phone in a drawer while you are working.

Of course, you can decide to take advantage of your freedom by seeing friends more. Meeting your friends on their lunch breaks can be a good way to avoid cabin fever feeling and is always appreciated. Or maybe you want to work in the morning and in the evening so you can spend the afternoon with your family. Just make sure that this is pre-planned and that you have a strict cut-off time for when your break ends and be consistent with that. You can give yourself a day off as well if you want to accept an invitation but realize that this is a bigger commitment. You will have to make up for that work elsewhere and then it will be hard to get back into your routine. Moreover, if you bend your rules a few times, people will expect you to do it every time. While it might not feel like it, being a bit strict and unsociable in the short-term will actually allow you to spend moretime with family and friends in the long run.

CHAPTER FOUR

Enhancing Your Health and Performance

Now that you have optimized your work-life balance and put systems and structures in place to define your work hours, you should find that you have a lot more time and energy for working. You should be less stressed and less tired. This is the structure that will allow you to build a truly healthy and optimal lifestyle. What you need to know is that your performance at work and your general health are closely tied together. The happier and healthier you are, the better you will perform when you are working. The better you work, the more time you will have to focus on your health. And it all starts with good night sleep.

Optimizing Sleep

By applying a little discipline, you will find that you less often allow your work life to ruin your sleep. This is criticalbecause your output will be significantly neutered if you don't sleep well. At the same time, you also need to ensure that you are doing everything to make your sleep the best it can be. For most people, this means going to bed at the same time every night and targeting to get a full eight hours sleep. Again, this is sacredand it will make allthe difference to every other aspect of your life.

Going to bed at a particular time every night is what will help you set your internal rhythms while waking up at the same time will prevent sleep inertia (and likewise prevent you from sleeping during your working hours). Make sure that your room is pitch darkand that light is kept to a minimum. Tape over the LEDs in the room and use heavy curtains to block prevent sunlight. To avoid 'blue light', don't look at your phone or computer beyond 8.00 PM. Caffeine should also be avoided after 4.00 PM and note that alcohol can ruinthe restorative nature of your rest.

A warm shower before bed can make a big difference to your sleep, as can stretching and meditation. Meditation is a great tool for encouraging mental discipline so that you are not thinking about work. Make sure you get adequate exercise and fresh air during the day so that you will be "tired" in the evening and will want to rest. Nutrition is also critical for healthy sleep and specifically, you need to be consuming enough vitamin D, magnesium and zinc to optimise your deep sleep.

Exercises

Exercise is a very important tool for the self-employed. Remember, working from home means you have no commute and that means less exercise. At the same time, it means you have at leastone hour you can commit to exercise in the morning and this will help to boost your brainpower. Exercise triggers the release of Brain-Derived Neurotrophic Factor (BDNF) which increases learning, plasticity and attention. It also helps in blood circulation to your brain and improves mood and focus. All these are wonderful tools for boosting your performance and combating health problems. Also important as well is stretching. Stretching boosts IQ and can prevent mobility issues that come from working on the computer. Yoga is a particularly good exercise but you can benefit by simply doing some stretches on a mat prior to lifting weights.

Now you may have a desire to look like Arnold Schwarzenegger. In which case, you need an entirely different book. But for purposes of optimal productivity and good health, you don't need to go crazy in the gym. In fact, it is better you don't. In its place, focus on exercise that is enjoyable and that you will stick to. Your aim here is to moveregularly and to apply a bit of positive stress (eustress) to your body to wake it up and strengthen it. Bodyweight training is good for this, the same way as running. Ultimately, it is better to have a very easy training regime that you can stick to, than an intense one that you never do. And in this regard, it is pertinent to find a gym that is near you or to set up your own gym at home. If the gym is 10 miles away and requires driving, it will eat into your day andyour energy level.

Nutrition

This is the most important of all: getting the nutrition right. Again, our aim here is not to turn you into Superman. Instead, it is to make you generally healthy, happy and able to work well. Avoiding obesity is part of that, so you should cut down on your carbs. Likewise, avoid carbs and sugars because they can make you tired after your blood sugar has spiked. Focus on filling up with complex carbs, fats and proteins and do not overeat. Working from home means you can eat smaller snacks instead of big meals and this is also prudent.

The most important thing to remember is that your diet should be nutrient-dense. This means you should focus on getting lots of fruits, vegetables, meats and more. The benefits that zinc, potassium, sodium, vitamin C, B complex, lutein, calcium, vitamin D, iron, omega 3 fatty acid, oils and more have on your body cannot be overstated. If you are getting your RDA of these, you will sleep better, feel happier, think faster and stronger. And the effects are more profound than any 'health supplement'. The best way is to eat lots of berries, fish, fruits, leafy greens, meats, organ meats and so on.

Do not cut anything out from your diet. Do everything you can to give your body a diverse and comprehensive selection of nutrients.

Introducing Kaizen

All this might sound too much to take all at once, but if you are creating a business plan that supports these changes, you will find it is much easier. The changes you make to improve your health and energy will feed into your work life and the improved work-life will feed into better health and energy. It is a virtuous cycle and that is why it makes sense to change everything at once, rather than viewing your 'diet' or your 'fitness' as isolated matters. But if it still sounds daunting, consider the concept of kaizen. Kaizen means making a small change in lifestyle that will have ripple effects on every other area. If you cannot change your diet immediately, commit to having a smoothie first thing in the morning. Or just do 20 press-ups in the evening. This change can lead to a healthy and happy entrepreneurial you that you want to become.

CHAPTER FIVE

Creating Your Home Business

Now you know how to manage your time, energy, workload and your clients, and you shouldbe happier, healthier and more productive as a result. You can now put your lifestyle first and your career second, and that is what working from home should really be about. But it will not be of much use if you are not already working from home. So, if you are still working in an office and are now ready to start your home-based business, this chapter is for you. This section would show you how you can set up more side-projects, and how you can adapt your current business model into something more conducive to a healthy lifestyle. With that in mind, here are some basic business models to consider.

Home Business Models for Lifestyle Design

If you want to work on a computer, there are different services you can provide online that are in high demand. Popular choices include web design, programming, graphic design, photography, copywriting and marketing. There are also others: you can offer proofreading services, virtual assistant services, consultation, legal advice, publishing, product design, social media management and lots more. You could even become a talent agent – most jobs nowadays can be done online. To start this business, all you need is to place an advert somewhere or respond to an advert. There are many places online that make this possible.

Warrior Forum and Digital Point Forums, for example, are forums frequently visited by website owners and digital marketers and you should be able to find lots of work there. You can also find work by posting on outsourcing sites like *Fiverr.com* and *Upwork.com*. *People Per Hour* is another good one. You can also try calling or e-mailing business owners or handing out business cards and going into stores! This has the advantage of being straightforward – you get paid for the work you do. At the same time, it is less scalable and not passive. It also means you will be rathertied to the schedule of those you are working for.

Publishing

You can make money as a website owner, blogger, YouTube vlogger or any other kind of online publishing. To do so, you have to build the popularity of your website, sell ad spaces, find sponsors or sell a product (either your own, or affiliate product for commission). All these are effective, and they are very good at bringing in residual income. The only downside is that you have to put in the work in the first place and it can take a while to start making money. A good compromise position is to try to earn money from a service while using this time to gradually build a website.

Selling Products

You can sell other people's products for commission (affiliate marketing), you can sell e-books from your website, you can sell an app, and you can sell the products you buy. To do the latter, all you need to do is find a cheap way to buy items in wholesale. Find a wholesaler or look on eBay and order your t-shirts, CDs or whatever else you want to sell in bulk. If you get about 100 to start with, it will not cost you toomuch and of course, you can sell them for more than you paid for each one individually.

Conclusion - Making the Leap

This all sounds well and good but there is a good chance you won't go for any of these models. Why? Because you are too scared to give up your day job. The good news is that you don't have to quit your day job. In fact, the better way to go about this is to start with a small business and slowly grow it in your free time (as a hobby) and then quit your job when you have enough work. Take two weeks off work, for example, and try finding some clients to do marketing for. If you find them easily enough and they seem to be offering steady work, then you can hand in your resignation notice.

Or start building a website on your lunch break and on weekends. It should be fun and something you will enjoy. If it starts making money, you can then work less and eventually quit your job altogether. Bear in mind that you need to approach this plan seriously if you want it to work out. If you are serious about earning a living from home, don't come up with an elaborate plan to make the next Facebook. That might work, but it is not a very reliable short-term strategy for improving your lifestyle. There is no need to reinvent the wheel, just go with a business model that has worked and execute it flawlessly.

And very importantly, make sure that when you do this, you also think about the lifestyle you want and howthat business is going to help you achieve that lifestyle. Think about your health, your sleep and your stress levels. Can your business model support the lifestyle you want to achieve, or are you still stuck in the opposite?

www.ingramcontent.com/pod-product-compliance
Lightning Source LLC
Chambersburg PA
CBHW070843220526
45466CB00002B/877